Look After Yourself

Healthy Eyes and Ears

Angela Royston

Heinemann
LIBRARY

www.heinemann.co.uk/library
Visit our website to find out more information about **Heinemann Library** books.

To order:
 Phone 44 (0) 1865 888066
 Send a fax to 44 (0) 1865 314091
 Visit the Heinemann Bookshop at www.heinemann.co.uk/library to browse our catalogue and order online.

First published in Great Britain by Heinemann Library, Halley Court, Jordan Hill, Oxford OX2 8EJ, part of Harcourt Education. Heinemann is a registered trademark of Harcourt Education Ltd.

Editorial: Sarah Eason and Kathy Peltan
Design: Dave Oakley, Arnos Design
Picture Research: Helen Reilly, Arnos Design
Production: Edward Moore

Originated by Dot Gradations Ltd
Printed and bound in Hong Kong and China by South China

ISBN 0 431 18026 1
07 06 05 04 03
10 9 8 7 6 5 4 3 2 1

British Library Cataloguing in Publication Data
Royston, Angela
Healthy eyes and ears. – (Look after yourself)
1.Eye – Care and hygiene – Juvenile literature
2.Ear – Care and hygiene – Juvenile literature
I.Title
612.8′4

A full catalogue record for this book is available from the British Library.

Acknowledgements
The publishers would like to thank the following for permission to reproduce photographs: Bubbles p.**9** (Anthony Dawton), p.**10** (Frans Rombout), p.**23**, p.**24** (Lucy Tizard) p.**27** (Claire Patton); Chris Honeywell p.**26**; DK Images pp.**4**, **22**; Eyewire p.**25**; Getty Images p.**6** (Ghislain & Marie David deLossy); Last Resort p.**12** (Jo Makin); Powerstock pp.**5**, **7**; Science Photo Library p.**11** (Adam Hart-Davies), p.**14** (Mark Clarke), p.**16** (BSIP, LECA); Trevor Clifford pp.**13**, **15**, **17**, **18**, **19**, **20**, **21**; Trip/Picturesque p.**8**.

Cover photograph reproduced with permission of Bubbles/Pauline Cutler.

The publishers would like to thank David Wright for his assistance in the preparation of this book.

Every effort has been made to contact copyright holders of any material reproduced in this book. Any omissions will be rectified in subsequent printings if notice is given to the publishers.

612.84

Contents

Words written in bold, **like this**, are explained in the Glossary.

Your body

Your body is made up of many different parts that work together. Skin, hands, eyes and ears are just some of these parts.

This girl sees the cat with her eyes. Her ears allow her to hear it purr. This book tells you how to look after your eyes and ears.

Your eyes

Your eyes are **delicate**, so you must look after them. **Eyelashes** and **eyelids** protect your eyes. They help to stop dust and dirt getting into your eyes.

Some people's eyes do not work as well as other people's eyes. If you have glasses, make sure you wear them. They will help you to see better.

Protect your eyes

Sunglasses protect your eyes from the Sun's rays. These rays can damage your eyes. Never look directly at the Sun, even through sunglasses.

Does the water in the swimming pool make your eyes sting? Swimming goggles help to protect your eyes from the water. Goggles also allow you to see underwater.

Eye tests

An eye test checks how well your eyes can see. A nurse or an **optometrist** carries out an eye test. She uses special glasses to test each eye.

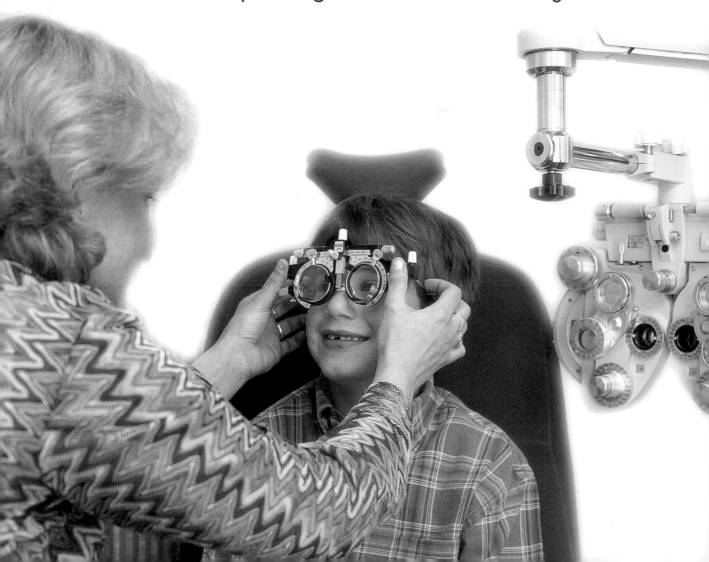

Some people can only see clearly things that are close to them. Others can only see things that are far away. The eye test shows if you need to wear glasses to help you see better.

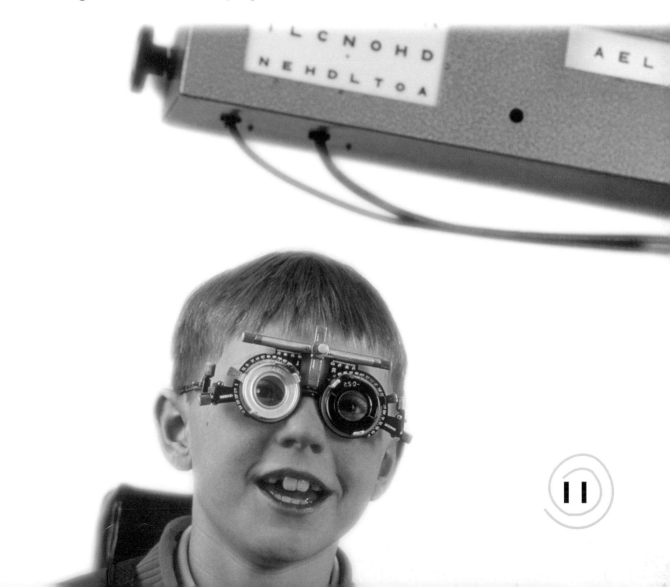

Getting dust out of your eye

Sometimes an **eyelash** or a speck of dust gets into your eye. It makes your eye sting and hurt really badly! Blinking fast helps to push the speck out.

Your eye makes extra **tears** to get rid of the speck. The tears should wash the speck right out of your eye. If they do not, ask an adult to help you.

Itchy eyes

Sometimes your eyes may itch. Some people are **allergic** to cats, house dust, or the fine **pollen** from flowers. The fine dust can make their **eyelids** red and swollen.

Germs can make your eyelids itchy too. Do not rub your eyes if they itch. You will only spread the germs to other parts of your eyelids.

Conjunctivitis

Conjunctivitis is a condition that makes your **eyelid** and your eye red and sore. If you think you may have it, you should go to a **doctor**.

One way of catching conjunctivitis is by using someone else's towel to dry your face. The **germs** can pass from the towel into your eyes.

Your ears

You can only see the outside of your ear.
Most of your ear is inside your head.
Sound travels down the **ear
canal** to the **eardrum**.
It goes through the
eardrum to the rest
of your ear.

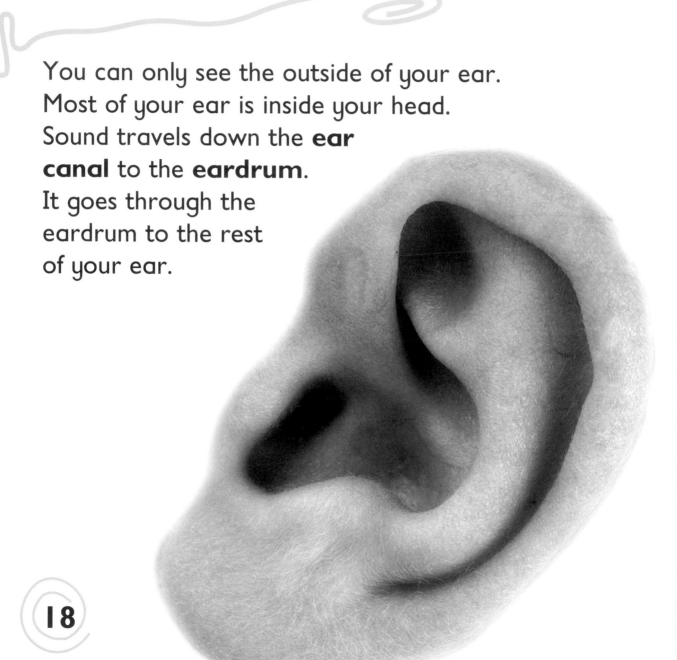

Your ears are complicated and **delicate**. They allow you to hear quiet noises and loud noises. Some noises are quiet because they are far away.

Look after your ears

Never put anything except ear plugs into your ears. Ear plugs keep water out of your ears when you swim. Other small things can get stuck in your ear.

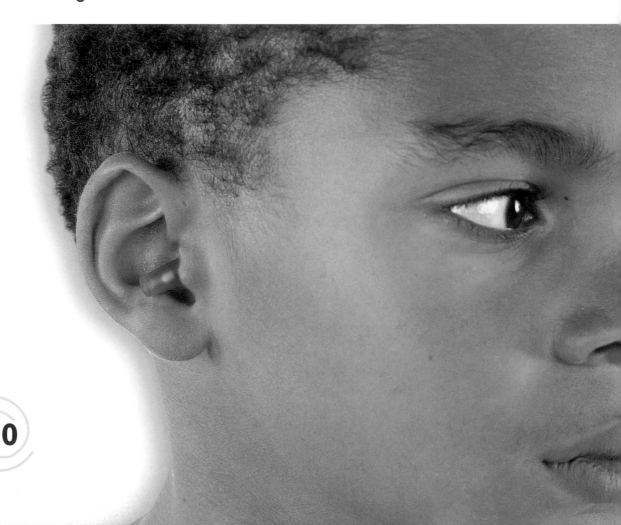

Dry the outside of your ear only. Your ear makes **wax** to trap dirt. The wax slowly pushes itself out of your ear. It doesn't need your help!

Hearing tests

Some people cannot hear as well as other people. They may not notice that they cannot hear well. All children should have their hearing checked regularly.

If you cannot hear well, you may need ear drops or a small **operation**. Some people have a **hearing aid** to help them hear better.

Earache

Your ears may ache sometimes if you have a cold or other illness. If the inside of your ear becomes infected with **germs**, it can hurt a lot. You may even feel dizzy.

Do not ignore earache. If taking a **painkiller** does not stop the ear aching, you should see a **doctor**. The doctor will look inside your ear and may give you **antibiotic** medicine to kill the germs.

Protect your ears

Very loud noises can damage your ears. If you are listening through headphones, make sure the music is not too loud.

Do not turn the television up too loud. If you often listen to very loud noises, your ears will not be able to hear very quiet noises.

It's a fact!

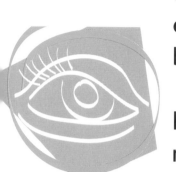

Salty water in your eyes helps to keep them clean. Every time you blink, your **eyelid** acts like a windscreen wiper because it washes your eye with water.

Blinking is the fastest movement you can make. You blink every few seconds without thinking, to cover your eyes with water.

Rubbing your eyes when you have **germs** on your fingers is the most common way of catching **conjunctivitis**. Since you never know when you might have conjunctivitis germs on your fingers, the best way to avoid conjunctivitis is not to rub your eyes!

Sound is measured in **decibels**. A normal conversation is about 60 decibels. A CD player played loudly on headphones is about 90 decibels.

Noises that are louder than 90 decibels can damage your ears. If a loud sound hurts your ears you should block your ears with your fingers.

People who work with very loud drills, chainsaws or other loud machines wear earmuffs to protect their ears.

Glossary

allergy   when the body reacts to something as though it were a germ, although the same thing is harmless to most people

antibiotic   medicine that kills bacteria

bacteria   tiny living things. Some types of bacteria can make you ill.

conjunctivitis   infection that affects the inside of the eyelids and the covering of the eye

decibel   unit used for measuring the volume of sound

delicate   easily damaged

doctor   person who knows how to treat illnesses and other things that may go wrong with the body

ear canal   passageway that leads from the outside of your head into the eardrum

eardrum   area of stretched skin inside your head that lets you hear sound

eyelash   hair that grows from the edge of the eyelid. It helps to stop dirt getting into the eye.

eyelid   fold of skin above and below the eye that partly covers the eye. The upper eyelid opens and closes to uncover and cover the eye.

germs   tiny forms of life that cause illness

hearing aid   small machine with a microphone that makes sounds louder. People who cannot hear well often wear a hearing aid.

operation   when something is done to part of the body, usually a part inside the body, to help it work better

optometrist   person who carries out eye tests and advises on the correct glasses

painkiller   drug that helps to stop pain

pollen   fine dust produced by flowering plants, particularly by grasses and some trees

tears   drops of water that spill from the eye

wax   sticky yellow substance that is made by the skin in the ear canal

Find out more

Body in Action: Seeing by Claire Llewellyn (Black, 2003)

Eyes and Ears by Simon Seymour (Harper Collins, 2003)

It's Catching: Conjunctivitis by Angela Royston (Heinemann Library, 2002)

My Healthy Body: The Senses by Veronica Ross (Belitha Press, 2002)

Safe and Sound: Healthy Body by Angela Royston (Heinemann Library, 2000)

Why Do My Eyes Itch? by Angela Royston (Heinemann, 2002)

Index

Titles in the *Look After Yourself* series include:

Get Some Exercise! Hardback 0 431 18020 2	**Get Some Rest!** Hardback 0 431 18021 0	**Healthy Eyes and Ears** Hardback 0 431 18026 1
Healthy Food Hardback 0 431 18019 9	**Healthy Hair** Hardback 0 431 18025 3	**Healthy Skin** Hardback 0 431 18024 5
Healthy Teeth Hardback 0 431 18022 9	**Keep Healthy!** Hardback 0 431 18027 X	

Find out about the other titles in this series on our website www.heinemann.co.uk/library